Found In
Grandma's Attic

Found In
Grandma's Attic

BONNIE HUDDLESTON IVEY-NOBLES

Library of Congress Control Number:		2022900169
ISBN:	Hardcover	978-1-6698-0543-4
	Softcover	978-1-6698-0541-0
	eBook	978-1-6698-0542-7

Print information available on the last page.

Rev. date: 01/10/2022

To order additional copies of this book, contact:
Xlibris
844-714-8691
www.Xlibris.com
Orders@Xlibris.com
838174

From The Author

by Dr Bonnie Ivey

We learn much from going through someone's attic. Oh, you say, "My house has no attic."

So wrong are you! I am 83 years old --- never lived in a house that had an attic. But I have an attic filled with many secrets --- the attic of my mind, my memories, my secrets, my self-talk that I would never verbalize to another human.

My self-talk is put on paper. Here are some secret things found in Grandma's attic. Things she could write but never say. Did not really know her until today.

Dedication

This book is written for and dedicated to my family:
Millie Swan, daughter; Ivey Bell, and Zoey Swan, granddaughters;
Millicent Bell, great granddaughter;
Charles Nobles, husband who had no idea this
book was written and being published and
to the memory of deceased loved ones, especially
to wonderful parents, Robert Lee and Barbra Alice Huddleston.

Dr. Bonnie Ivey, Ed.D

Summary of experiences: **Teacher, counselor, social worker, therapist:**

29 years experience in Lauderdale, Newton, Itawamba, Washington, Jones, Forrest and Lamar Counties and Tuscaloosa, Alabama; State Child Abuse Investigator for State of Mississippi; Habilitation Therapist working with mentally challenged persons.

Business experience as manager, secretary, bookkeeper, printer, pageant director.

Education **December, 2007 Doctor of Education, Ed.D. Ed. Leadership Nova Southeastern University, Fischler School of Education and Human Services Miami/Ft. Lauderdale, Florida**

Master of Education, M.Ed. Vocational Rehab.

Counseling Mississippi State University, Starkville, Mississippi

B.A./ Sociology/S.W. Mississippi State University, Starkville, Ms.

A.A. Business E.C.J.C., Decatur, Mississippi

Diploma from Beulah-Hubbard High School, Little Rock, Mississippi

Other: Mississippi University of Women, Columbus, Mississippi. Business Education

University of West Alabama, Livingston, Alabama, Creative Writing

Ms. State and Meridian Community College, Meridian, Ms., Elementary Education, Math, Children's Literature, Reading

Certificate of Theology, 2009, Grace Communion Seminary, Glendora, California

Completed Master of Pastoral Ministry, Theology degree 2013, Grace Communion Seminary, Glendora, California

Image of Loveliness Course, Joan Wallace, Oregon

Bronze Medal in Arthur Murray Ballroom Dancing

Chaperone for American Theater Abroad Bye Bye Birdie Broadway Show Cast; London, England School of Ballet and Modeling; Barnhill Theater, University of Exeter, Exeter England,

Professional — **Numerous memberships throughout the years**

Phi Gamma Sigma

Ms. Retired Association

Life member Ladies Auxillary VFW Meridian, MS Post

Languages — **Signing, and 12 Semester Hrs. in Spanish**

References — **upon request**

Extra-curricular Activities: **Numerous from sponsorship to committee member: Modeling Squad, Clubs, Classes, Croft, Church Deaconess and Church Treasurer**

Accreditations — **Class 4-A** Ms. Teacher Licensure: H.S. English, Social Studies, Bus. Ed., Home Economics/Consumer Ed., Guidance Co., Child Care, Psychology, Bible

Awards received — **Who's Who, Dean's List, Poet of the Year, Tom Tom News Editor, Several Mrs. Pageant winnings**

| Publications: | Dissertation: Locus of Control; Columnist for local newspapers, Best Poet of the Year, State Curriculum Lesson Plans, High School Editor, College Editor, Teen Progressive Farmer Essay. Published in Mountain News |

Dr. Bonnie Ivey

Retired teacher, S.W., Counselor, Therapist

Hattiesburg, MS 39404
iveybonnie63@gmail.com - 601-549-6626

Having retired from the Mississippi State Department of Education I seek to continue use of my skills agreeing to negotiate salaries and benefits. My main interests are in fields of education, counseling and human services. I am educationally and experientially qualified for diverse employment as a team member yet self-motivated and capable of working without supervision. I will be a viable asset to any organization or company.

WORK EXPERIENCE

Habilitation tx tm coordinator II
Partlow - Tuscaloosa, AL - 1990 to 1992

Responsibilities
I supervised teachers for educational retarded residents, wrote tx plans, conducted staffing and did on call shifts. I was involved in meeting Certification defects as the hospital was on probation caused by a situation years before I went to work there.

Accomplishments
I made corrections. I made awareness of Needs to improve aides direct care.

Skills Used
Counselor. Administrative. Leadership. Therapist.

Ellisville St School and East Ms St Hospital as social worker and counselor
state institutions for mentally ill and retarded - Meridian, MS - 1987 to 1991

Responsibilities
Wired on acute ward doing intake social histories. Did group and individual counseling. Wrote treatment plans. Coordinated services and did placements. Worked with families. Did staffing and and assisted doctor's evaluations along with much paper work and on call responsibilities.

Accomplishments
I was successful in bringing clients to optimal level of functional abilities.

Skills Used
Social worker training. Psychology and counseling qualifications. Communication skills. Record and progress notes and social histories using written communication skills.

Teacher, Counselor, Therapist, LSW,
Retired Mississippi State Dept. of Ed. - Jackson, MS

My work experiences include teaching, counseling, director of out-patient mental health clinic; M.H. therapist; licensed social worker and state child abuse investigator, managerial positions; legal and insurance offices, executive secretarial and bookkeeping positions.

I have taught elementary and high school students. I have been on staffing committees, worked with the gifted as well as the severely retarded/handicapables and the acutely mentally ill as counselor, teacher, therapist, case manager, facilitator of individual and group counseling. I have taught parenting skills and programs to potential foster parents as well as teaching parents who wished to have their children returned to home. I participated in court hearings involving my clients as an expert witness.

SKILLS

- Educational skills
- Communication skills, written and oral
- Computer skills and office machines: switchboard operator; off-set printing; Dictaphones
- Typing at 80/WPM; Shorthand at 120-200/WPM; Ten-key adding machines by touch
- Multi-cultural skills
- Teaching skills
- Team work skills as leader or follower
- Multi-talented skills
- Motivational speaking skills
- Maturity

I have 4-A Level St. of Ms. Teacher Certification in the following: English, Soc. Stds, Psy, Child Care, Home Ec., Bus. Ed., Bible

EDUCATION

Ed.D in Education and Human Services
Nova Southeastern University - Fort Lauderdale, FL

B.A. & Masters - Counseling
Mississippi State University - Starkville, MS

Creative Writing
Mississippi University for Women - West Alabama, NY

Ms. Rehabilitation Center - Coordinator

SKILLS

all business machines such as dictaphone; switchboards; adding machines; posting; computers; printers; shorthand and typing; filing; payroll; ads; executive secretary; legal secretary.

SOON THE PAIR OF HANDS OF THE FIRST
GENERATION WILL BE REMOVED.
THEN ANOTHER WILL MOVE TO SPACE.
EACH SET WILL CONTINUE NOURISHING'S, WIPING OF
TEARS, CATCHING FALLS, GUIDING STEPS, BANDAGING
KNEES, GIVING LOVING TOUCHING'S, FEEDING
HUNGRY MOUTHS, BUT MOST OF ALL, FOLDING
HANDS IN PRAYERS FOR ALL WHO GROAN IN HIS
ENDING TIME OF A SIN-FILLED WORLD AWAITING
THE KINGDOM OF GOD RULED BY JESUS AS KING OF
KINGS FOR A PEACEFUL WORLD. "COME QUICKLY"

Nannie's Technology

By Dr. Bonnie Ivey

I have a new computer today
gonna learn come what may
and it will be a long way
typing what I wanna say

I am an old lady you see
although slow I may be
just sit back and watch me
I am busy as a bumbling bee

Climbing Mountains

Dr. Bonnie Ivey

Climbing, Climbing, Climbing--
Tired and weary,
Up a step, down two,
Summiting, Summiting, Summiting--
I head toward peaks bare and pointed,
Assaulted by storms and tempest.
Frosted fragmenting rocks
Tumbling, Tumbling, Tumbling--
Ignorant of nature's power.
I, the modern woman,
Unlike independent mountain man
Sustained by she-goat's milk
Continue without advancement
Until I hear a loud voice
Roaring, Roaring, Roaring--
"Never try to go straight up a mountain.
Wind upward like a spiral staircase,
Taking rest stops I have carved."
Resting, Climbing, Continuing...
Learning more the long way up!

Reaching, Looking, Seeing
From God's view;
Knowing His presence
Is on top of the mountain
And also in the valley below--
Wherever I dwell.

To thank you for my being able to smile again:

This is a song I wrote when I was a mental health therapist working with depressed elderly groups. I had them to sing it to the tune of AULD LANG SYNE. SING IT!

A Smile

By Dr. Bonnie Ivey

A Smile is such a magic thing

It changes your whole face

But one it's gone, it's hard to find

The secret hiding place

How wonderful it is to see

What one small smile can do

I smile at you, you smile at me

And one smile makes two

    I had them sing it and then laugh until a handkerchief I would drop hit the floor. The one who laughed the loudest got a prize.

    It was a good lung exercise as well!

Have a great 2018!!

ok nanny here is your poem:

Little Sheep of the Field

Little sheep of the field
Yes, they have much to learn
Lying there in their flock
Winking at me with sleepy eyes
Dreaming of peaceful meadows they have grazed
And cool English streams under bridges
And their shepherd's rod gently guiding.
They know their master's voice
These little sheep of the field.

By Bonnie Ivey

Fireworks of God

By Dr. Bonnie F. Ivey-Nobles

The thunder roars.

The lightning flashes.

The wind soars.

The rain splashes.

There is a knock on the Ark.

Too late to come in.

Should have knocked before dark.

You were busy laughing then!

Early Mornings

by Dr. Bonnie F. Ivey-Nobles

My Daddy poked the logs before daybreak

And with shivering hands

He warmed a sheet to wrap me.

I WAS NEVER COLD

NEVER COLD!

I would sit on his lap with his arms around me

And with calloused kind hands

He tied my high tops one by one

I WAS NEVER BAREFOOT

NEVER BAREFOOT!

Next he would take his thin blade pocket-knife

And with nurturing hands

He split the mellowed apple

And scraped it with a spoon for me

    I WAS NEVER HUNGRY

        NEVER HUNGRY!

Did I say, "Thank you"?

I don't remember

I did not know he was cold

I did not know he was barefoot

I did not know he was hungry

    THANK YOU DADDY

        THANK YOU!

Confessions

by: Dr. Bonnie F. Ivey-Nobles

Tell me everything and know I forgive

I willingly died for you to live

Don't think I will love you less

If you have life's mistakes to confess

From Law to Grace

by Dr. Bonnie Ivey-Nobles

Without God's Holy Spirit, there had to be Law made.
Physical correction was all man could understand.
Even then, His Law was not obeyed.
Few listened to God's voice.
Others made another choice.
God forgave and forgave,
Holding fast to the promises made to those few.

The pitiful sinful state of man
Called for God's saving grace,
And sacrificial plan.
He emptied Himself to be in man's place,
The payment of man's sin.
The Devil will never win.

Earworms

by Dr. Bonnie Ivey-Nobles

Do you have a worm in your ear?
    Can't you hear what I have to say?
Look at me. Bring yourself near.
    Your night can change to day.

That jingle keeps going round and round,
    Inside your head, can't get it out.
Until your head begins to pound and pound.
    For your attention, I must shout.

Won't you remove that worm in your ear?
    Do you know there is a way?
There is nothing for you to fear.
    Then you can hear what I have to say.

June 9, 2020 - A Tuesday AM 8 AM

Come Quickly

I need you every breath I take
Thank you for giving me that breath
Thank you for giving your life for my sake
I will watch for your coming til my death

Through many trials you have kept me from harm
Thank you for planning a peaceful time
Thank you for your Word sending an Alarm
Through all the dangers Satan made look fine

Not far away
Comes the day
You will stay
Satan will pay
Jesus rules - hooray

Alone

by Dr. Bonnie Ivey

I did not sigh or cry
Because alone was I
   But tried to keep a servant's heart
By always doing my part
   Then came along this man
Who was not at all in my plan
   Trusted him and loved him
Then learned I was only his whim
   So now again I'm the fool
While he without conscience is cool -

He puts on his narcisstic charms
Claiming just wants to be nice
But at home with wife he harms
So he can controls she pays the price

His words are spoken out loud & clear
Later proclaims that you just made it up the days
As he denies what he said without fear
Knowing God watches from up above always

A perfect example of how he makes wrong right
And makes right a wrong giving Satan Delight
For Satan, the father of liars since Eve

Finally provoked to anger hurt deceived from being abused
Tired of being a maid and totally misused
I will fight him & his for my sight
And he can stay in the dark running from God's light

Safety

by Dr Bonnie Ivey

I sit in the warmth
steaming from the sunlit sky
with tears of joy cooling
my cheeks.

It is like being nearer to you
Oh God wrapped in your
warm & loving arms.

Motivation

by Dr. Bonnie Ivey

A glimpse of morning
Alerts me to a new opportunity

I feel a song in my heart
 But I cannot sing it for you
I hear music in my heart
 But I cannot play it for you

I see beauty all around myself
 But I cannot open your eyes to see
I smell sweet aroma in my nose
 But I cannot emit it to yours
I taste marvelous flavors on my tongue
 But I cannot satisfy your taste buds
God must call you to feel,
 to hear, to see, to smell, to taste
I cannot but pray

Silent Talent
by Dr. Bonnie Ivey

Come Quickly

by Dr. Bonnie Ivey

I no longer am content
   to imagine you
I want to see you face to face
Although I shall tremble
   at your sight
Come soon, come soon. Tonight?
Fulfil the promise to your Son
give Him your kingdom
with his co-heirs for which
He bought with His blood.
   I claim to be an unworthy one
Owing many accounts
Yet am debt free
Cause you pd them for Me -

Upward

by Dr. Bonnie Ivey

Look to the sky so high -
See many stars - why?
Needed to meet necessary light
Only one would give a dark sight -

Awakened

by Dr. Bonnie Ivey

Good morning to you my loving God always
Then many nights of sleeping, you extend my days
With opportunities to be more like thee
Oh how I want to like you to be
Thank you for a choice of wrong or right
Results of choosing your way is worth the fight
Keep me always in the battle to win
Overcoming this lost world of sin

"No Footprints Behind Me"

by Dr. Bonnie Fay (Huddleston) Ivey

Stepping to the right. Stepping to the left. Stepping backward. Stepping forward.... sounds like dance steps and indeed it is -- to the rhythm of life circling round and round in the same place at times and circling the entire floor at other times, tiring, forced to sit out and wait for the slower step. Then suddenly stepping on a slippery spot, tripping but rescued by my dance partner catching me and getting me back in step hiding my clumsiness.

Forgotten

by Dr. Bonnie Ivey

Said he had forgotten
No surprise
Makes me feel rotten
Is loving him unwise?

Because he chose to forget
My heart is a grave for my love
Will there be a resurrection Day?
Should I stay or go away?

Distant Love

by Dr. Bfi

It is so strange
Knowing you are far away
Yet I feel you within range
As my love grows stronger each day

If ever we meet eye to eye
I know we both will agree
We will never say goodbye
Together we will always be

So let me dream of us each minute
Waiting for tomorrow to appear
Having to cope without you in it
Forgive me if I must shed a tear

I'll keep waiting for you to arrive
Depending on secret dreams to stay alive
Imaging your arms are opened wide
Where I can be forever by your side

Do Not be Afraid

by Dr. Bfi

Yes, I love you today
But do not run away
I ask no return of love, you see
Because I know you can't love me
I'll just be your friend anyhow
One day you will find your love
Hopefully sent to you from Him above

Confessions

by Dr. Bonnie F. Ivey

Tell me everything
Don't think I will love you less
Because you have life mistakes to confess
I take you for better, for worse please see
And proudly recall promises from me
Tell me everything but love only me-

Tears

by Dr. Bonnie F. Ivey

Tear drops
like cold winter rain
wet my pillow tonight
and washes away sleep.

But a glimpse of morning
alerts me to a new opportunity
as tears of joy and warmth
streaming from a sun-lit sky
dry my wet soaked cheeks
wrapped in your loving arms

Yesterday or Today?

by Dr. Bonnie Ivey

Today will be yesterday
That day that went away

Todays never will stay
Those days pass, come what may

Consequences will remain
Some are joy, some are pain

Wisdom is seldom the gain
Like opportunitie on a missed train
Past yesterdays lived in vain

Tears

by B. Ivey

Tear drops
like cold winter rain
wet my pillow tonight
& washes away sleep

But a glimpse of morning
alerts me to a new opportunity
for tears of joy & warmth
streaming from a sun-lit sky
Drying my wet soaked cheeks
wrapped in your loving arms

Come Go With Me To My Father's House

"Where does your Father live?"   (In my heart)

"Is He alone?" (am I?)   (Never)

"How old is He?"   (He hasn't told)

"Do you live far from Him?"   (a prayer away)

"Are you His only child?"   (No, indeed)

"When can I meet Him?"   (Your choice)

"Can I go alone?"   (definitely)

"How long can I stay?"   (Eternally)

"What should I wear?"   (a white robe)

There is no B.C. - Christ Jesus
has always been & was
before human form -

The funeral of love

There lay the corpse
cold and still
w/o a chance to heal
all the emotion sealed within
too dead to feel again

He Fooled

By Dr Bonnie Ivey

My name is Bonnie
Once he called me honey
When our love was so sweet,
Just talking was a special treat
The sky was beautiful, so blue
We promised love always true
Then somehow I did not fill his need
Although I tried to succeed -
Will he have enough to gain
I surely hope his next will be true
One who loves him as much as I do

To justify, causing another pain
As he called himself single
Again going on FB to mingle

Only time will reveal
Which love is real -
And was his freedom of choice
Better than listening to God's voice?

There lay the coupe

There are tears of sadness
      tears of gladness
      tears of pain
      tears remain

Tears give comfort & relief ease
Tears when down on one's knees

Can You Still

Open eyes that still can cry, see
    spine or backbone to be responsible
open lips that won't lie
    legs that walk away from evil
open ears that can hear
    or
have arms that can give hugs

have lips that will kiss
conscious that turns away from wrongs

have a heart that can romance

have feet that can dance

have a nose that can smell flowers

have a brain that can think

have hands that can hold

have priorities based on God's Word

Never take a fence down until you
know why it was put up.

Being loved by all
is no fun
unless much loved by one

a small look can sink a ship

You have to do your own growing
No matter how tall your grandfather was

Trying to conceal wounds that haven't healed
is foolish

Your choices & actions reveal your character

Dig the well before you are thirsty

To know the road ahead; ask those who are coming back

A bad workman blames his tools

after the horse is out
why close the gate

A sleepy fox catches no chickens

Anacisstic's Wife

by Dr. Bonnie Ivey

I no longer am confused
In denial, no longer I see
Have been too long an object abused
No respect, care or love for me
Just meant to serve & be used

Four years waiting for a change
Ends only in more hurt & pain

May 31, 2020 - Sunday
Annual Holy Day of Pentecost

I will follow God
even though I do not
know where He is taking me -

These are photos of those
who I spent the happiest
days of my life

Luke 7
John 11

Belief is not faith
Faith is only good as
what one has belief in.

Faith in God is not valid if one does not know Biblical Jesus

Expectation is belief in future of God's plan

Enemy of faith
worry fear doubt reason of self

Hope of word
He will create

Hope in future

Gives confidence to submit to God

Faith is being humble before God

Faith motivates
pleasing God with obedience

Last nights the stars were hidden
Thunder was roaring, storms were near
   For safety, and mercy God was bidden
He heard and removed doubts and fear -

   Tonight God reveals the moon He just lit
Darkness is no longer all around
   Thankful hearts feel safely securely fit
Fall asleep not hearing a sound

Morning comes with warmth of the sun

I must tell you while I still can remember. Let me talk. Let me babble.
Let a tear roll down my cheek. Let me also laugh & smile. And you
never forget I love you and I prayed for you

This morning is so foggy
I kinda feel groggy
Inside I want to stay
Can't go out and play

So now what shall I do
Right now I have no clue

I'll sit by the phone
Yes, all alone

Terese
"Love Begins
Taking care of those close at home"

May 1, 2018

Multi Billionaire w/ no Bank Account

By Dr. Bonnie Ivey

It isn't money I own
Nor a mansion for my home
I live day to day
Waiting for God to show the way
Sometimes I must fast
When the food doesn't last
If the elec bill is too high
A candle is always near by
So if the water is cut off at the same time
God sends the rain and all is fine.
No money in the bank? Is ok you see
God is my billionaire Father taking care of me -

"Mama"

by Dr. Bonnie Ivey

I was sick in bed,
When mama said:
"I'm going to see granddad."
It made me so mad.

Why leave me I cried
As I clung to her & sighed
All effort to not leave me, I tried
Is she coming back or just lied

Now as I look back, I see
She had to see grandpa for me
Mama begged for the doctor's fee
There she returned to me speedily -

God's America to Give

by Dr. Bonnie Ivey

A land owned by the Creator of All
His to give to His chosen to be free
Freely He gave His Only Son for me
Abraham obeyed God of creation
He was promised a mighty nation.

Brick Walls

by Dr. Bonnie Ivey

How Satan loves throwing bricks
Trying to hit God's select
Yet to His surprise those bricks
Are used to build a wall
Between them Satan's tools
They never got hit at all
Between them Satan's Tools
So who really rules?

The more bricks thrown at me
The bigger the wall goes up, you see?

Run, flee Satan, go on your way
Your bricks won't hurt me, your time has run out
Your day is near the time you'll pay
Bound in chains, go pout
Groaning w/ pains w/ fire so hot
Look what you got!

God's Sheep

by Dr. Bonnie Ivey

Look at God's sheep
    So well fed
To green pastures
    They are led

Look at God's sheep
    So well protected
From dangers faced
    Never are neglected -

Look at God's sheep
    So well aware
Of their shepherd's voice
    Never w/out his care

Sept. 16, 2018 - 4am - Sunday

Non Committal

by Dr. Bonnie Ivey

I was happy as could be
Thinking he would commit to me
But the Narcistic ego was seen
As he flirted w/ store clerks like a teen.

Then I could understand why
Only he would go to certain stores to buy
Denying me a wife's right to choose
When I suggest locally grown food I lose -

He cannot go shop without attentions
Thinking he is friendly he mentions
It is an obsessive narcistic need
For narcistic's attention's as feed

May 2, 2018

#

No Chance
By Dr. Bonnie Ivey

Never in all my eighty years
Have I shed so many tears
Married legally to a narcistic man
Never, never was in my old age plan

But here I sit emotionally abused
Only fitting where I can be used
He threatened to even take my life
I'm never treated as a wife.

He wants to appear to others so nice
While alone w/ me I pay a price.
Praying to God to keep me safe as I wait
Hoping, knowing His answer will comes before too late

Creative fiction based on Career experience

UNNOTICED ONES HIDING

Dr. Fay began her group session as the way she had done so for the past several years, cheerfully greeting each one she found waiting in the recreation room although everyone except John Lee paid her no attention:

"Morning, Dr. Fay! I've been waiting on you. You gonna let me go home today?"

"Not today, John Lee."

Dr. Fay sat down in the only vacant chair in the circle and checked her roll. With all ten accounted for, she was about to give each one a sheet of paper with a drawing of a person without any facial features drawn on it, when John Lee jerked them from her."

"I will assist you today, Dr. Fay", exclaimed John Lee as he began to pass a sheet to each person in the circle.

"Thank you, John Lee. Now please give each person a pencil for me."

As John Lee passed out the pencils, Dr. Fay explained that she wanted each of them to draw a face on the person showing how they were feeling at the moment. She drew a face on her sheet showing a smile and explained she was happy to be there with all of them.

Each finished his picture. John Lee proudly held his picture up before the group, explaining:

"I drew my mouth downward and upward because I am happy to have Dr. Fay to talk to but I am sad because she won't let me go home today."

"What would you do if you were home today?", asked Dr. Fay.

"I'd drive my car to Mom's Café and eat breakfast. Then I'd go to see my Honey Bun. We'd go on a picnic and swim in the lake. That's why I wanna go home....to see my Honey Bun. Can't I go today?"

Bob Lowe spoke up. "You do not even have a Honey Bun. You do not even have a car. You do not even have a home to go to and if you left here today, you would be back on the street, drunk and stinking."

Bob Lowe held up his picture. He explained that he drew his face with tight lips because he is tired of taking medicines that are not helping at all. He told the group he would not be taking them when he gets home. "I am going to get me a good glass of whisky and forget all them pills."

And you would be trying to kill somebody again. That's why you ain't never getting outa here, man", piped in Tom Tew. "Now look at my face I drew. I put glasses on him and a very serious look because I will be going back to my office and with my intelligence and education, I'll be making money practicing medicine. I'll have so many patients when they get word that I will give them pain killers as long as they say that they hurt."

"Well", Packer Paul answered. "How will you get away with that? You lost your med license practicing that way and you were taking as many pain killers as your patients you killed. Man you are crazy! Now, look at my picture. You see me with closed eyes and smiling. I had a good night's sleep last night and I had happy dreams of dying and going to Heaven. I think God is telling me I'm going to die right here and nobody but Him will notice I ever lived."

Everyone suddenly was silent. Then Jim Barr stood up and began explaining his picture. "I drew mine with a cigar in my mouth. I'm dying for a smoke. If I could get ground privileges, I'd pick up all the butts on the ground and smoke all day long. Dr. Fay, can't I get off this oxygen long enough for one cigar?" Levon Love chimed in. "He's gonna die anyway. He already has liver cancer from all that alcohol he drank." Holding up his picture, Levon Love showed his picture. He had drawn his person wearing a hat with a large feather. "I want to dress up and go to church Easter Sunday and when I walk in, the whole bunch of hypocrites will notice me. I know the Bible front and back and every time, I went to church back home, I was not allowed to preach or even comment during services. They totally ignored me. The preacher was not interpreting the scripture right."

Lewis Lord was rocking back and forth in his chair. He had drawn nothing. Dr. Fay asked, "Lewis, would you please show us your picture?" Without answering, he held up his picture with a blank face. He said, "I drew nothing cause I don't feel nothing." Harry Horn responded to Lewis. "You fried your brains and look at you. You pathetic soul, blind in one eye cause you tried to dig it out. Well, I do feel something and I am glad. See my picture. I drew tears down my face. I want to cry and never stop. I can't get my mama off my mind, seeing her hanging by a rope in our barn and it was all my fault for not taking care of her."

Nolan Nash jumped to his feet and angrily told Harry: "You know you are in denial that you are the one who beat her and hanged her cause you didn't want her to send you here to get help. But you had to come anyway, didn't you?" Nolan proceeded to share his drawing with a big smiling face showing big teeth. "I drew a happy face. Today, I am going to the dentist and get some teeth."

Everyone laughed because they knew his teeth got knocked out by a man who caught him in a motel room with his wife.

"Well, be sure you put your new teeth in your pocket the next time you are fooling with a married woman," stated Larry Lile as he held up his picture saying: "Well here's my drawing. I drew a big, wide-eyed face cause I can see why I am in here and nobody wants me around. These scars on my arms from self-mutilation ain't nothing compared to the scars on my heart. I just want to die when I think of my stepdad doing to me what he did. I tried suicide. I was stopped, but I will do it when nobody is watching."

Dr. Fay had hurriedly written notes while each man presented his picture. After Larry finished showing his picture, the session's time was up, so she handed out another sheet to each man instructing them to draw the face showing how they would like to feel and bring to the next session ready to explain what it would take to feel that way and do brainstorming.

Name: Dr. Bonnie Ivey-Nobles
Date: March 27, 2018
CAPSTONE PAPER ASSIGNMENT - Part Two
For Master of Divinity Degree Requirement-- TM 501
Grace Communion Seminary
Professor: Dr. Michael Morrison

PTSD

by Bonnie Ivey

"Sleep with a marine," they say, "if you want to be safe."

Lou lies in bed every night beside her marine husband, a 100% disabled Korean War Veteran. She feels safe, yet has dodged his flinging fists to avoid black eyes. She has not slept a night through in years. He pounds the headboard of the bed. He mumbles in his fitful sleep. He suddenly sits on the side of the bed time and again throughout the night. Lou's side of the bed slopes and she sleeps on a hill. The mattress sags from his weight, 300 lb.

The days are like living in a morgue. He breathes, but lies in his recliner like a corpse, eyes closed, sleeping, hallucinating, insisting on a darkened room. Each doctor's visit, he is given higher doses of meds sedating him into total inactivity. He eats well. He weighs 310 pound. He grunts with every breath when Lou is in his presence.

Lou asks herself, "Am I safe?" She wonders: Is he just lazy? Does he have mental problems that were undetected before becoming a marine? Lou has been told that Post Traumatic Stress Disorder results from constantly being on alert in the war zone programming the synapasis to remain on alert. The mood swings. The paranoia comes and goes. Tears easily flow at any news about war. Each morning he complains of a new pain and informs Lou again and again that he will die soon -- the last pain, he thought he had bought the farm. (Lou hopes it takes her as long to die as it is taking him. For a number of years, he has claimed it would be his last alive.)

If only she could get him to do something = anything, but getting him to even take a bath is like trying to move a brick wall. He declares he is not depressed, just physically unable to do anything. Yet, the heart is functioning okay, oxygen level okay, BP okay, can eat anything.

He never accepts responsibility for anything, never considers Lou and her arthritic body, her emotional well-being. There is no escape for her. She spends every hour being nurse, caretaker housekeeper, cook, & financial manager. Is she safe? Who will take care of her?

So give to the VA, but nothing for her is on the way ---- must stay or go without pay –

Next Dance

by Bonnie Ivey

Zeffie sat with three other wall flowers. Although the chairs were quite comfortable, she twisted and turned trying to sneak glances toward the punch bowl where Johnny stood holding a drink in each hand. She wondered if he were waiting for Zola to come from the powder room. Zeffie decided to go to the powder room also and just as she stood up, she saw Johnny walking toward her.

"You look thirsty so I have a drink for you."

"Yes, I was about to go to the punch bowl. Thank you. Guess you must be a bit thirsty -yourself after all those dances with Zola."

"She had to leave early -- has an early work day tomorrow."

"Lotta pretty ladies here tonight. Now you can dance with all of them."

"I only want to dance the rest of tonight with you. Ready"?

Johnny took her hand, but she thought she would not look too anxious. She gently withdrew her hand, smiled and answered:

"I need to make a quick phone call. I'll be back shortly and the next dance will be ours."

Johnny watched her stroll across the room toward the powder room. His thoughts raced back to the first time he met Zeffie. Her hair had not begun to grey then. She was still grieving over her husband's tragic death in a motorcycle accident. They had been married thirty years, deeply devoted to each other --- had no children. She was in the Greyson Hotel lobby waiting to have lunch with his sister, Irene. They had been acquainted since their college days, but he had been in the army, traveling all over the world until he retired this past January, so he had not met Zeffie until that day. His sister had asked him to drop by the hotel to pick up tickets to the upcoming football game she had for him.

His thoughts were interrupted by Zeffie's return just in time to catch the next dance -

HOW SCRIPTURE AND THEOLOGY HELPS ME:

This study of Scripture and Theology has helped me in many ways. Theology is a part of my growing Christian life and proves that my life is not meant to be only a biological existence. As I study, I become more and more aware of the importance of self-reflection. Biblical assessment of Theologians must be based on Scripture to stay focused on truth found only in the Word and the only place to learn who God is and His relation to the world is in His inspired Word opening minds by the Holy Spirit Jesus left us to guide us after His human earthly departure. The pages below will give only a portion of all I have gained from seeking this degree.

More insight and depth has been gained by studying the person, the life, the work, and ministry of Jesus Christ Who reveals the Father and left us the Holy Spirit. Each study session has been beneficial as Scripture has given revelation of a future when the church age will end. The Bible Scripture is an excellent way to learn about human nature. The study of what God is doing and has done to redeem humankind throughout the history of His creation explains that salvation is available to all. Theology involves the study of sin and the consequences to individuals and nations worldwide.

So much is involved in the study of Theology and Theologians that subjects will never be exhausted. Learning how the Church began, what the Church is and is not, what and how leadership must be today to witness Biblical truth is also gained by Biblical theological study to understand what I believe and why I believe as I do. I learn how to correctly divide the Word. (II Tim. 2:15). With more Biblical study, it is easier for me see how Christianity differs from other religions not Biblically proven.

Paul warns all to be aware of sheep in wolves clothing, false teachers, vain traditions of men who are not of Christ. (I Pet 3:15, Jude 3, Matt. 7:15, Col 2:1-4, 8) To be able to prove the spirits, a study of angels and demons is necessary. An understanding of a heaven and a hell judgment is necessary to understand prophecy.

A study of God's Word cannot be exhausted. Everything studied leads to a new study and as all over-laps, all fits into a whole understanding of God, Who He is, and what He is doing as He prepares a place for us to live with Him forever.

INSIGHT OF JESUS AND PAUL:

Some argue that Paul and Jesus gave conflicting messages which is Biblically not true. Paul fulfilled Jesus' ministry. Jesus taught the Kingdom of Heaven and Paul taught justification by faith. Each of them was an example of a servant's heart. They taught that one who is a member of any church not founded by Jesus has no promise of eternal salvation.

Jesus is the founder and foundation, the corner stone, of the Church of Christ. (I Cor. 3:11) Both Paul and Jesus warned about false teachers. Both focused on the Trinity. As the Father loves the Son and the Son loves the Father powered by the Holy Spirit, we are shown the out-going and in-coming flow of love. An understanding of "I Am" is prevalent although the mystery of the Trinity cannot be totally comprehensive to us because it goes beyond our human reasoning. Not everything can be explained because some secrets belong to God.

Both Jesus and Paul knew our humanness and understand what we want to do, we do not do. Jesus died for us knowing we could never pay all the debts we owe. His grace is freely offered, and it is up to all to accept or reject. There is no basis for thinking Jesus and Paul gave teaching that opposed one another. Their lives were witnesses to Jew and Gentile people.

HOW I SEE MY ROLE:

I cannot emphatically say that I see my role as any one role. I have been basically a lay member, a deaconess, a volunteer, a director of women's ministry and acceptor of any opportunity to serve as called on by Pastors.

The roles of the ministry are fast changing daily whereas in the past, churches had only one Pastor who was sole leader. Today, a team of elders and a board make decisions as well as having membership voting. Staff members do the caring services resulting in more training needed from universities and seminaries. (Apologetics and all religions of the world need Biblical truths that are being denied more and more.) The churches in my area have a minister for every service they provide. A senior pastor is done away with for fear of not showing equal authority to all. Many social and community programs necessitate having more ministers. Requests for counseling is handled by lay members with counseling credentials. The pulpit is used to focus more on growth than providing nourishment for the already members. The minister of music with a band uses more church time for praise and worship than is used for sermons to edify the congregation.

As I researched the above facts, I find that with my education and experiences, I could qualify for any role, but my gifts from God are not presently being utilized in a church. Privately, I welcome any opportunity to serve anyone that God allows in my path. I am sought by those who need a listener and need input to help clarify their situation with choices to relieve their burden. For example, an elderly lady who knew my Dad, phoned me weeping and scared because her elderly husband had expired and had never been baptized. She told me she could not find an answer from anyone that gave her peace. Her husband did not attend any church although he believed in Godly living and was a loving neighbor. She had heard all her life that one had to be baptized or if died and had not been, would burn in a hell fire eternally. I knew one community church pastor who would pound his fist and at the end of his sermon shouted out that short and long graves were in the cemetery inferring that his hearers might die at any time without baptism and be lost. Then as he begged any down the aisle, the choir sang "Oh Why Not Tonight". The fear tactic scared some into false conversion thinking they got saved when a minor child or older whenever they joined the church.

With the Holy Spirit guiding, I gave her Scriptures to reveal God's plan of salvation showing that all will be given a chance to accept His Truth and few would end up denying Him. She also had never been baptized and feared for herself. She later phoned and said she had found mental peace. She died shortly afterwards also.

So reflecting on such as this situation and other such times, I filled a need such as sitting with a critically ill person, taking elderly ones to shop who had no relative to assist them, or directing a wedding for those who could not afford one otherwise, or arranging baptisms at my home, or babysitting for a family, or just putting flowers or water on the podium, etc., etc., am I to see myself as a counselor, teacher, or caretaker, or a Jane of all trades?? I can only pray for guidance to witness God's love and truth to any coming before me and thank God for any opportunity to do so. I do not need a "role" to do so if I ask for a servant's heart.

BIBLICAL CHURCH IMAGES SHAPING WHAT I DO:

The Church is my pillow and my grounding of faith. The church age as we know it began after Jesus was on earth. (I Tim. 3:15, Matt. 16:18). Jesus built His church. He is the founder and foundation. (Psm. 127:1, Matt 15:13, I Cor. 3:11)

The Holy Spirit came to the disciples to preach languages so all could understand. Three thousand were added. (Acts 1:1-4, Acts 2:37, 38, Acts 2:41, 47). The church came with power. (Mark 9:1). It was the Church of Christ, not of John, the Baptist! Paul established churches throughout the Roman Empire, in Europe and beyond-- even in Africa. They were little flocks and persecuted during the period of emperors Nero, Domitian, Diocletian. Constantine came on the scene proclaiming conversion and called the First Council of Nicea doing a codification of Christian faith. Afterwards was the Council of Chaldean and then the Nicene Creed as still used today confirming belief in God, Christ and the Church.

A split between the Eastern and Western Christianity came about. The Filioque controversy over who sent the Holy Spirit caused a final split. Things like arguing over use of leavened bread for Passover and Easter, or how often to do communion or the Trinity caused divisions. The church not in unity and not displaying love for one another prevented shining forth. (I Cor, 1:10). When Martin Luther came on the scene, splits from the Catholics took place. History shows a Protestant take-over of England. Protestants split over baptism, salvation, Jesus' nature, ambiguous scriptures, leadership, female roles, religious services, gays and lesbians, ordinations, and church membership. etc., The arguments that blame the divided body of Christ on theologians, church rulers, and politicians continue to exist. I am amazed that in all the books written on the history of the church never or seldom is there discussion of the history of how pagan beliefs and traditions of men became part of today's Christian celebrations that the Bible condemns.

All mentioned above make it very difficult to sort out and to not be influenced by unless diligent study of the Word is prayerfully studied and guided by the Holy Spirit. All the written histories of the church cannot refer to the true Church of Jesus. If so, then there would be only one denomination.

Allow me now, to discuss the Biblical images of the Church of Jesus that I focus on to avoid the common image of a physical building. An actual temple is depicted in the Old Testament, but now God's people are the Temple of God and in them is where the Holy Spirit dwells. The Book of Revelation reveals the image of a lampstand to shine a light in a dark world not knowing God. Another image is one of being a Bride showing God loves the collective body as a husband loves a wife by promises of protecting and providing needs, willing to die for her. The family is another image of the Church. God is Father, brethren are brothers and sisters who love one another. The older teaching the younger. The Church is depicted as the Body of Christ with a head, hands, feet and body parts to show diverse roles, gifts, and differences--the head being Jesus.

These images teach me we are to love one another, care for one another, and are to know individually our bodies are the dwelling place of God's Holy Spirit. I can understand that when the Church is referred to, it is not a building. In Acts, Paul strengthened the Church, greeted the Church, visited the Church--people not a building in each case. In Timothy the Church is to help widows and orphans which refers to the people, not a building. The Church people are to shine and witness to spread the Gospel--not a building shining! Instead of saying: "I am going to Church", I am learning to say I am meeting with God's people at a certain location!!

I have gained insight from each course I have taken while pursuing this degree. I respect all the diverse interpretations of the theologians but do not agree with every wind of doctrine which motivates me to search God's Word more diligently and prayerfully asking the Holy Spirit to open my mind to His Truth and expose my personal biases, background, and mis-interpreting I must abandon. The most troubling teaching I read and hear from pulpits is explanation of what happens at baptism and at death. I have searched and cannot find any reason to teach that when one is baptized, they are saved at that moment. Nor can I find anywhere in the Bible that when one dies, one goes to Heaven to be with God and will return with Jesus. I read of three resurrections of three different categories of persons. I read that the dead are as asleep with no consciousness until they are resurrected. Jesus ascended to the Father after he was resurrected. Why would Jesus not tell the disciples what He experienced while in the grave and if He had already gone to the Father why would He say He had to ascend to the Father. I do not read that spouses will reunite with their mate in Heaven as is taught by certain churches. I read of no male/female or marriages in Heaven among spirit beings. I read that death ends the physical marriage contract. What role one will play during the one thousand-year period is for God to decide. Unless the Bible interprets the Bible, error will be taught. To not add to or take from the Bible is not to be done. Therefore, where the Bible is silent one should be silent. Can one find an apple tree if given the description of a banana tree?

RECALLING RESEARCH AND AUTHORS INTRODUCED IN THIS CURRICULUM OF STUDY:

The most recent texts have included Derick Tidball's "Ministry by the Book" from which I was guided through his models for the ministry concluding with his encouragement to pastors to not just conform to the dysfunctional models of leadership by realizing that the New

Testament models enable freer choices because not one model fits all due to backgrounds and needs differing.

The text, "Exploring Ecclesiology" written by Brad Harper and Paul Louis Metzger presented a study of what the church is and what it is not and questioning if one does not know what the church is, how can one know what it should do. The focus was on a Trinitarian Church, the sacraments, a serving community and cultural aspects including discussion of female roles.

In Ray S. Anderson's book, "The Shape of Practical Theology" shows a Trinitarian approach for the practice of ministry regarding the concerns minister face. He does not avoid discussion of any situation found in the congregations. His discussions of female roles and homosexual's need are included which expands Christian counseling. His case studies help clarify his attempt to combine theology and the ministry. I developed more compassion after having read this book; however, it will take me several re-readings to grasp more of the importance of all Dr. Anderson presents.

The study of the book, "Exploring Ecclesiology", (a study of what the Church is) by Brad Harper and Paul Louis Metzger enlightened my view of the issues so relevant in today's prosperity and consumerism preaching. The beginning chapter focused on the Church as Trinitarian which gave me a deeper understanding.

Dr. Gary Deddo's lesson given on Barth's theology regarding personal relations has been part of studying that gave me even more insight about the Trinity so debated by church groups. Even demons understand the three persons are in perfect unity. The demons shudder. (James 2:19)

There has been so much new and old learning and review that overlaps, I am overwhelmed trying to condense all of it into a comprehensive capstone. The professors such as Dr. McKenna, Dr. Morrison, as well as authors I have been introduced to via of the course work required for this degree has resulted in my growth cognitively and spiritually. I am unable to relay it all back without rambling. I understand now why I felt authors were guilty of rambling back and forth. Then I come to see all parts came together to reveal a whole concept. A little learning can be a dangerous thing. It is wise to gather all the facts to come to the right conclusion in any matter. Without doing so when interpreting Scripture, one will be taking the situation out of context and using false reasoning. The Bible warns us of how worldly scholars will not be the spiritually wise.

Church leaders are Biblically deficient in some cases and their theology is linked to emotions having no understanding of interrelations of the Trinity. Ordinations include the novice members who have not matured as leaders. This is a situation exists often and to resolve such would require observing one prayerfully who is being considered for ordination asking for guidance of the Holy Spirit to reveal matured readiness and Godly calling.

I have been motivated to do deeper study into the different forms of worship focused on different aspects. For instance, the Pop-Contemporary follow whatever makes them feel good, the Traditional includes reverence with concern about how to worship, the Corporate focuses on the family meeting with God, and the Christian worship is Trinitarian keeping God-centeredness and Scriptural guidelines and Christ-based. I continue to search the New Testament and find no reference to worship or praise methods of worship and praise. True worship and praise is of the heart, not seen in action or words. Paul described orderly worship for God's glory. I search to find the basis for publicly bowing silently at an altar before a congregation. I do not find public prayers that sound like a person's private prayer that would be more appropriate in one's closet done in secret as the way to pray in a public setting. I do not understand focus on self rather than God if gathered to give praise to God. The book of Psalms is seldom used or sang. There is much to learn from the study of Job, more than self-righteousness so commonly focused on. Is all this avoidance caused by Pastors staying "in the box"?

I want to continue much more study to learn the value of each method, whether it changes lives, teaches Biblical Truth or merely entertains. Does one go forward or backward in understanding.

As I end my capstone assignment, I will give a fun approach regarding the pun on words used for justification of interpretations. This way, many "prove" what they want the Scripture to say to keep from changing their traditional beliefs. One can make the Bible say what one wants it to say if one does not allow the Holy Spirit to guide allowing the Bible to interpret the Bible and keeping Scripture in context.

PUNS ON WORDS:

These are just fun examples to bring attention to the importance to study to be approved and know false teachers:

Who is the most flagrant law breaker in the Bible? Moses broke all ten commandments at once. Which Bible character had no parents? Joshua, the son of Nun. What kind of man was Boaz before he married? Ruthless. Which area around Palestine was so wealthy? Probably around Jordan where the banks were always overflowing. Who was the greatest Biblical comedian? Samson. He brought the house down. Who was the greatest babysitter? David. He rocked Goliath into a deep, deep sleep. Who was the greatest female financier? Pharaoh's daughter. She went to the bank of the Nile and drew out a little Prophet. Who was the very greatest financier in the Bible? Noah. He was floating his stock while everyone else was in liquidation. Did God call Pastor's in Germany German Shepherds? On and on words can be used to convey truth or mis-information. To prayerfully study to prove all things is the important re-enforcement my study for this degree has given me.

Concluding, I cannot list the hundred books I have read to satisfy the pursuit of this degree, nor all the research articles along with deeper Scriptural reading. All the theologians and religions motivated me to learn more from God's Word. I have at times felt misplaced among God's Pastors when I have had trouble discerning how to do assignments since I am not a Pastor. Then I was guided to I Corinthians 12:12. Here I see that every believer is a member of Christ's body with a definite ministry. The body parts each have a function only that body part performs and is necessary for the whole body. For instance, if the body were only the body part of an ear, how could there be sight. The body has many members for a different service. Because I am not a Pastor of a church does not mean I have no ministry. My response to the assignments differ from the Pastor which has God's purpose as He has chosen. The theological lens that help me keep focus is the image of God. I keep focus on my belief not being just an intellectual exercise but it is my way of life that affects how I pray, worship, and relate to God and to one another as a Christian.

The course work is ending, but not my continuation to study to show myself approved. Happenings each day are proofs of our Creator, His Word, His love and His plan unfolding. I realize how much I need Christian brethren in my life for encouragement to keep running the race. Most of all that I have learned from this course is that I love Him for including me in His plan and I ask each night: "Did I do anything today that only a Christian would do"?

"How Humans Are Like Sheep:"

Sheep love sheep.
They are friendly/social
They enjoy growing together in small groups.

Sheep are timid and panic easily
They need a shepherd to protect from wolves and winter time
They cannot survive in the wild like other animals

Sheep have no sense of direction
They wander off and cannot return without being brought back
They cannot swim

Sheep cannot get up if they fall need shepherd to help them up-
They know their masters' voice.
They need water, but will hover over an empty trough and need their
shepherd to lead them to water.

Interesting:

Owners of sheep paid a price for them and looks for any lost to not lose
the price they paid.

(Jesus paid for us -- His sheep -- and does not want to lose any)

The shepherds rod and staff is
used to guide safely not to beat them, but fends off wolves and harmful
things

Hunger and bugs make sheep restless.
Hungry sheep will eat anything

A bug nestles in the sheep's head and if their shepherd does not see the
bugs, bugs will multiply and will blind the sheep eventually

Olive oil on a sheep's head stops bugs from landing on the sheep's head The devil is called Beelzebub who is the Lord of flies. Bugs are symbolic of demons

Annointing of Holy Spirit protects us from being harrassed by demons!

CPSIA information can be obtained
at www.ICGtesting.com
Printed in the USA
LVHW051111020322
712194LV00006B/222

9 781669 805410